Fresh Island Style

Fresh Island Style

Casual Entertaining and Inspirations
from a Tropical Place

Alicia Rountree
written with Caitlin Leffel

Foreword by Glenda Bailey
Photography by Dewey Nicks

Rizzoli
NEW YORK

New York Paris London Milan

To my parents for raising me in an environment full of magic, and for teaching me that through hard work, imagination, and dedication, anything is possible.

Foreword

There's a certain type of woman we'd all love to be: stylish, self-possessed, and certain of what we have to offer to the world. In these ways—and many others—Alicia Rountree is a true inspiration. She is effortlessly chic, standing apart not just because of her statuesque beauty but because of the way she exudes the serenity of an islander in everything she does. But it is in her work that Alicia truly shines. From her role as the co-founder of Tartinery, the Paris-by-way-of-NYC café chainlet that celebrates fresh food made from real ingredients, to her ingenious collection Alicia Swim, which makes bikinis using regenerated nylon from discarded oceanic fishing nets, to the magic she has wrought in the pages of this title, Alicia is defined by her dedication to helping others find balance through a healthy lifestyle.

In that respect, *Fresh Island Style* is a great achievement. It is more than just a tome on inspirational living: whether you reside in Mauritius or Manhattan—or points in between—this is a book that reminds you of the magic to be found in slowing down and savoring the small moments of life, from the bright, juicy flavor of a fresh pineapple to the gradient beauty of a sunset over water. We may not all have the opportunity to call an island paradise home, but we can all stand to learn a thing or two about taking stock of what's around us—and taking the time to soak it all in.

With its sumptuous full-color photographs and mouth-watering recipes from Alicia's own personal collection, *Fresh Island Style* is a feast for the senses. In between shots of turquoise water so bright and deep you'll want to stick your hand through the page, Alicia shares stories from her life and upbringing and divulges her secrets to maintaining balance as a busy entrepreneur. Alicia manages to make having it all look effortless, but she's not greedy about her secrets: she wants you, the reader, to achieve that same level of fulfillment. And all you have to do to get there is turn the page.

— Glenda Bailey

Introduction

When people ask me what it was like to grow up in Mauritius, I have a hard time answering—I don't have another childhood to compare it to. So I often start by describing what it's like to live on a tropical island.

Proximity to water is one of the most distinctive parts of island life; most of my childhood memories are set by the ocean rather than on land. When I was growing up, I used to water-ski before school, then jump back in the water for a swim when I got home. The sea has a huge influence on Mauritians, in many ways. We have a deep connection to ocean life, and most of us care very much about marine conservation, coral preservation (Mauritius is surrounded by ninety miles of coral reef), and the well-being of sea life in the Indian Ocean. This connection to water has also inspired my swimwear line. Because I literally grew up in a bathing suit—it is hard to find a childhood photo in which I'm not wearing one—I am truly more comfortable in a swimsuit than anything else. As you will see in the pattern illustrations throughout the book, the first prints I designed included ones inspired by coral and waves (along with leaves and frangipani, a yellow tropical flower that is found all over the island). And because the fragility of ocean life is always on my mind, I donate a portion of the proceeds from the line to the Mauritius Marine Conservation Society.

The natural beauty of my island home has long been sought after by visitors—"Mauritius was made first, and then heaven; and that heaven was copied after Mauritius," wrote Mark Twain after coming to the island in 1896—but the breathtaking landscape (which also includes rain forests, mountains, volcanic rock, and an energy vortex) is only part of what makes this island so alluring. Throughout this book there are images that show the beautiful intermingling of nationalities, customs, and religions that has created a uniquely warm and vibrant atmosphere. This cultural diversity combines with the lush variety of tropical fruits and vegetables in our cuisine. The recipes in this book include both traditional Mauritian cuisine (including *gato piment*, a staple of my family kitchen) and simple dishes of produce, herbs, and legumes that emphasize freshness over elaborate preparations.

This page and opposite: Scenes from my life at home. We're never far from the water, whether we are water-skiing, horseback riding, out on a boat, or spending time at the beach house on the south coast of the island (*page 20, top right*). When people visit, we always tell them that a few swimsuits are all they need.

When you are raised on a remote island, your world is naturally small and close-knit; a subtler aspect of my island life is a deep connection to family and home. For most people, Mauritius is an epic getaway; for me it is also full of quieter pleasures and simple, casual rituals: Sunday lunches with family, picnics on the beach, sunset dinners with friends. My parents are both native Mauritians, seven generations on both sides. They met on the island when they were young, then reunited in Mauritius as adults. The house I grew up in was a secluded, colonial-style home on a farm that has been in my father's family for many years. To get there, you leave the main road and drive through fields of sugarcane—which, when mature, can grow to be thirteen feet high—a journey that evokes a sense of being transported to a magical land. Some kids look forward to snow days; we looked forward to torrential storm days because it meant that the road would be too flooded to drive to school, so we would head down to the cliffs to swim in the rain. As a child, I had a pet lemur and my sister, at one point, had a baby monkey. (The lemur slept in the bed with me, curled up on my pillow, until my mother thought better of that sleeping arrangement because no one was getting any sleep.) Ducks, ostriches, and donkeys mingled with our more traditional house pets. Elsewhere giant tortoises roamed, and there were ponds filled with bright red and orange koi. There was always something new to discover, like a family of tenrecs (tiny hedgehog-like mammals) in the herb garden; a turmeric plant just pulled from the ground, displaying its vibrant orange root; or a piece of antique glassware, porcelain, or silver passed down through the generations. This peaceful, family-centric way of life, with little barrier between indoors and outdoors, was my world. I try to carry that sense of calm and groundedness with me wherever I go, and it inspires the style of living, eating, and entertaining that readers will experience in this book. When visitors come to stay with us in Mauritius, they often say that by the time they leave, they feel as though they've become part of the family—the highest compliment, I think, any guest can pay to a place they've visited.

This page, clockwise from top left: Striking an impromptu shoulder stand by the edge of the cliff in the wild south; detail of the lush exterior of the house I grew up in; one of the trains that used to transport cut sugarcane from the fields to the factories for processing. *Opposite:* The road to my childhood home, with fields of sugarcane on either side.

Fresh Island Style

This page and previous spread: The design of the guest house at the beach is more modern than the family home, but the white exterior and interior features such as the nautilus-shaped staircase (*opposite*) keep the mood light and airy. The beach is no place for a house that takes itself too seriously.

Fresh Island Style

Morning
on the
Dock

In Mauritius, I wake up with the sun. I leave the curtains open before I go to bed so that the first rays of daylight serve as my alarm clock. (When I'm away from the island, I try to find other ways to rise that are gentler than the alarm feature of my phone.)

The first thing I do each day are my morning pages. I keep a notebook and a pen next to my bed, and as soon as I'm awake, I write whatever comes into my mind. This practice isn't about coming up with something polished; it's about the process of chronicling unfiltered thoughts. I try to fill at least two pages, though some days I have more to say than others. Over time, I see patterns in my writing, and if I find myself coming back to the same subject over and over again, I know it's something I need to focus on.

Moving early in the morning is vital; the busier I am, the more crucial it is that I do some form of movement before I start working. I like to paddleboard at daybreak for a kind of moving meditation. The water is at its calmest at that hour, and I find that the gentle, repetitive motion helps me mentally prepare for the day. I also work in at least a few minutes of yoga. Even one or two poses (or a single sun salutation) is better than nothing.

Then it's breakfast time. I don't eat before yoga or paddleboarding—those are gentle exercises, better to be done in a fasting state. But as soon as I get home, I have some tropical fruit—papaya, mango, lychees—or a fruit juice, like watermelon. Juices are great in the morning because they are naturally revitalizing—their vitamins are absorbed right into the bloodstream. Then I might dig into one of my beloved coconuts, or if I need something heartier, I'll have an adaptogenic smoothie, or avocado toast, topped with a poached egg. I try to give my body whatever it needs in the morning to tackle the day ahead. I always make time to fuel properly and enjoy the food and the company of my family. That sets the day off on the right track.

This page and opposite: It's not hard to get myself out of the house at dawn when I know that it's the most peaceful time to be on the water—usually it's just me and the sea life. *Page 28:* I like to add an adaptogenic powder to my smoothies to boost whatever I feel I need that day: *maca* for energy, *ashwagandha* for well-being, or medicinal mushrooms for brain health.

Fresh Island Style

SMOOTHIES

EACH SERVES 1

In a blender, blend all ingredients on high. Pour into a tall glass and enjoy. Feel free to use either homemade (see recipe below) or store-bought almond milk, or a nut milk of your choice.

FOCUS SMOOTHIE

½ frozen banana
½ cup pineapple cubes
1 teaspoon freshly squeezed lime juice
2 Medjool dates, pitted
1¼ cups almond milk

CURE-ALL SMOOTHIE

2 frozen bananas
3 ounces spinach
1 Medjool date, pitted
1¼ cups almond milk
½ teaspoon spirulina powder

ENERGY ACAI SMOOTHIE

½ cup blueberries
¼ cup frozen acai puree, about
   ½ 3.53-ounce package
2 frozen bananas
¼ cup frozen dragon fruit, about
   ½ 3.53-ounce package
3 teaspoons coconut pulp
1¼ cups almond milk
½ teaspoon flaxseed

INSPIRATIONAL SMOOTHIE

½ cup frozen papaya chunks
¾ frozen banana
3 fresh strawberries, hulled
1 cup aloe vera juice
1 teaspoon probiotic powder

CALMING CHOCOLATE SHAKE

1¼ cups almond milk
2 frozen bananas
2 Medjool dates, pitted
1 teaspoon chocolate protein powder
1 teaspoon cocoa nibs
1 tablespoon coconut pulp

EASY ALMOND MILK

MAKES 4 CUPS

1 cup blanched raw almonds,
   preferably organic
2 cups ice-cold water

In a high-powered blender, process the almonds until they have a very fine texture. Add the water and blend on high until the mixture is smooth and creamy.

Store in the refrigerator in an airtight container for up to 4 days.

Note: Use ice-cold water straight from the refrigerator so the mixture won't be lumpy. You will not need a nut bag to strain the almond milk.

Fresh Island Style

29

AVOCADO TOAST
SERVES 2

2 slices Einkorn or other whole-grain
bread (see recipe on page 121)
1 avocado
2 tablespoons chopped cilantro
Salt to taste
Freshly ground black pepper to taste
2 thick tomato slices
½ cup loosely packed arugula leaves
Freshly squeezed juice of ½ lemon
1 tablespoon mixed seeds, such as
sunflower, flax, and chia
2 poached eggs (optional, see Note)

Toast the bread until golden and set aside.

Halve, pit, and peel the avocado. In a medium-size bowl, mash the avocado very roughly with cilantro, salt, and pepper.

Place the toast on a serving plate. Spread equal amounts of the avocado mixture on each slice. Add the tomato and a few arugula leaves on top of each. Drizzle lemon juice on top of each piece, and finish by sprinkling the seed mixture over both. Top with poached eggs, if using.

Note: To poach eggs, crack each egg into a teacup or a small bowl. Bring a saucepan full of water with 1 teaspoon of white vinegar to boil. When it is boiling, use a wooden spoon to swirl the water in a circular motion and gently slip the cracked eggs into the water. Lower the heat and cook gently for 5 minutes. Remove carefully with a slotted spoon or skimmer and transfer to toast.

Fresh Island Style

Page 30: Morning produce deliveries from our garden come wrapped in a latanier palm leaf. *Below and opposite*: Pineapple is great for boosting the immune system, while papaya aids digestion, and helps reduce inflammation inside the body. We often eat papaya with a squeeze of lime on top for extra Vitamin C.

A coconut can be a three-course meal! I start
by drinking the water; it's very hydrating and
replenishing after my morning activity or when
the sun is really intense. Next, I eat the meat—
my favorite part—straight from the coconut
with a spoon. Then I take whatever is left over
and save it for smoothies.

"There's so much goodness inside coconuts. I eat them raw, I cook with them, and I use the oil in my hair and on my skin. They are nature's version of a true multitasker."

Fresh Island Style

Family
Sunday

"Magical" is the word my mother uses when she describes the type of childhood she and my father wanted to give their children. Though we are now grown up with families and careers all over the globe, our attachment to Mauritius and each other has deepened over the years. So while it is hardly the most convenient meeting point on the planet, Mauritius is the place we always come back to, and where we all feel most at home.

We live all over the world now (London, New York, Kenya, and Australia, to name a few places). It is our priority to come together as a family as often as possible, and when we are together, gathering around the table for leisurely Sunday lunches is an important ritual. They are always casual affairs—this is Mauritius, so we're more than likely to be setting the table in a swimsuit and dining barefoot—which helps keep the focus on the thing we most treasure: simply enjoying one another's company.

One thing I like about these meals is that everyone chips in a bit, all the way down to my baby niece, Kiera, who will play at bringing us flowers and leaves and whatever she can find to decorate the table with. There's never one host or hostess, or a highly organized menu. Everyone brings a few things to eat or drink and once we've gathered, we work together to cook our favorite Mauritian dishes, make fresh salads and use vegetables from the garden, and set the table. In this way, the prep itself becomes a part of the get-together, and another way to enjoy each other's company.

Often the conversation leads to childhood memories, and sometimes we'll bring out some family photos to pass around the table while we reminisce. Somehow, no matter how many times we've done this, there is always a new story from my mother, or a new memory from a brother or sister that keeps us at the table all afternoon, until we realize that it is almost time for the next meal.

MOCKTAILS

WATERMELON MINT REFRESHER
SERVES 2

3 to 4 cups peeled, cubed watermelon
1 lime
5 to 6 fresh mint leaves
2 cups sparkling water
2 hibiscus flowers
2 sticks sugarcane

Puree the watermelon in a blender. Set a fine sieve over a bowl, then transfer the watermelon puree to the sieve. Press the watermelon puree through the sieve. Discard pulp and seeds.

Juice the lime and muddle the mint leaves in the lime juice. Strain and discard solids.

In a pitcher, combine the watermelon and lime juices. Pour in the sparkling water.

Fill 2 drinking glasses with ice and pour the drinks over the ice cubes. Place a hibiscus flower in each glass and serve sugarcane as swizzle sticks.

CUCUMBER LEMON DROP
SERVES 2

2 tablespoons demerara sugar
1 cucumber
Freshly squeezed juice of 4 lemons
2 cups sparkling water
2 strawberries

Combine the sugar and ½ cup water in a small saucepan. Bring to a simmer over low heat and cook until sugar is completely dissolved, about 2 minutes. Set aside to cool.

Chop the cucumber (unpeeled and unseeded) and puree in a blender. Set a fine sieve over a bowl, transfer the cucumber puree to the sieve, and let it drain for 15 to 20 minutes. Press the cucumber pulp against the sieve to extract all the juice. Discard pulp.

In a pitcher, combine the sugar syrup, the cucumber juice, and the lemon juice and stir to combine. Add the sparkling water.

Fill 2 drinking glasses with ice and pour the drinks over the ice cubes. Cut slits in the strawberries without going all the way through and use to garnish the rims.

Fresh Island Style

Fresh Island Style

We often mix colorful flowers with textural tropical foliage to decorate the table, in a way that looks wild and natural—not fussy or done up. If there are children around, picking the flowers together is a fun way for them to help get the table ready.

45

This page: Wrapping napkins with a bit of twine and a small bud is a nice, understated way to add an accent from the natural world to a table. *Following spread*: You can't go wrong with simplicity; a palette of blue and white is always elegant and goes with every menu and mood.

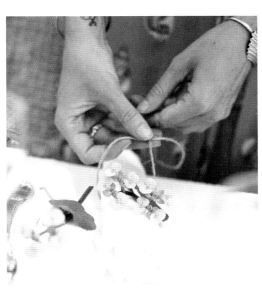

VINAIGRETTE
MAKES ABOUT ¼ CUP DRESSING,
ABOUT 2 SERVINGS

1 clove garlic, peeled
1 tablespoon apple cider vinegar
Pink Himalayan salt to taste
Freshly ground black pepper to taste
½ teaspoon grainy mustard
½ teaspoon honey
3 tablespoons extra-virgin olive oil,
   or more to taste

Crush the garlic with the side of a knife
blade. In a small mixing bowl, combine
all of the ingredients except the olive
oil. Mix well. Gradually whisk in the
olive oil to taste. Serve with a green salad.

COCONUT CURRY STEW
SERVES 4

1 12-ounce package dried rice noodles
2 tablespoons coconut oil
1 medium white onion, julienned
2 medium carrots, peeled and cut into thin slices
1 cup broccoli florets
1 tablespoon yellow curry powder
1 tablespoon soy sauce
6 cloves garlic, peeled and minced
2 tablespoons minced fresh ginger
1½ cups vegetable broth or water
3 cups coconut milk
1 pound spinach, chopped
¼ cup chopped cilantro
2 tablespoons freshly squeezed lime juice
1 teaspoon hot sauce
Salt and freshly ground black pepper to taste
Cilantro leaves, sliced scallions, and lime
   wedges for serving

Soak the rice noodles in warm water until pliable, at least 30 minutes. Drain and set aside.

Meanwhile, place the oil in a large stockpot over medium heat. Sauté the onion and carrot until softened, about 5 minutes. Add the broccoli and sauté for an additional 5 minutes.

Add the curry powder, soy sauce, garlic, and ginger and cook, stirring frequently, for 8 minutes. Add the broth and the coconut milk and bring to a boil, then turn down to a simmer. Stir in the spinach until wilted. Add the noodles, stir to combine, and cook until noodles are soft to the bite, about 2 additional minutes.

Remove the pot from the heat and stir in cilantro, lime juice, and hot sauce. Taste and adjust seasoning.

Serve hot with cilantro, scallions, and lime wedges on the side.

VEGETABLE AND PANEER CURRY
SERVES 4

1 2-inch piece ginger, peeled and roughly chopped
7 cloves garlic, peeled
½ small head cauliflower, chopped
1 eggplant, diced
1 medium zucchini, diced
½ cup diced squash
1 cup okra
2 tablespoons ground cumin
2 tablespoons turmeric powder
Salt and freshly ground black pepper to taste
¼ cup vegetable oil
2 medium yellow onions, sliced
1 large tomato, chopped
2 to 3 tablespoons Curry Paste (see page 53)
⅓ cup diced paneer
½ cup chopped cilantro

In a blender or a food processor fitted with the metal blade, or a mortar and pestle, grind the ginger and garlic into a paste.

In a large bowl, combine the cauliflower, eggplant, zucchini, squash, and okra with the ginger and garlic paste. Massage the paste into the vegetables. Sprinkle on the cumin and turmeric and season with salt and pepper. Toss to combine, cover, and set the vegetables aside to rest at room temperature for about 1 hour.

Heat a stockpot over medium heat, add the vegetable oil. Add the vegetable mixture and sauté, stirring frequently, until vegetables are browned, about 10 minutes. Add the onions and tomato. Cook, stirring frequently, for 10 minutes. Add the curry paste. If the mixture is so dry that it is sticking to the bottom of the pot, add about ¼ cup water. Stir in the paneer. Reduce heat to low, cover, and simmer until all the vegetables are tender, about 15 minutes. Remove from heat, adjust seasoning. Sprinkle with cilantro, serve.

CURRY PASTE
MAKES ABOUT 1 CUP PASTE

1 ounce dried whole turmeric

3 tablespoons toasted coriander seeds

3 tablespoons toasted cumin seeds

*3 tablespoons peeled and roughly
    chopped garlic*

*2 tablespoons peeled and roughly
    chopped ginger*

1½ teaspoons fenugreek seeds

2 tablespoons chopped red onion

8 to 10 fresh curry leaves, roughly chopped

1 small fresh green chili

Using a mortar and pestle, first crush the turmeric and then add the other ingredients one at a time in the order provided, grinding to a paste in between additions. Use immediately or transfer to a jar, add enough oil just to cover the surface, seal with a tight-fitting lid, and refrigerate for up to 1 week. The paste can be frozen for longer storage.

53

Fresh Island Style

"There is nothing more nourishing than a meal with family. A few simple dishes and a table set in a spot that you'll want to linger at are really all you need to feel comforted and grounded by one another's company."

Previous spread: When my family is together, we always make our favorite Mauritian foods—the dishes we grew up on that don't taste as good anywhere else. *This page*: Bringing out family albums is a wonderful conversation starter—no matter how many times we look at these pictures, there are always new stories to hear.

A Day
at Sea

The Mauritian equivalent of a road trip is a day at sea. When I have downtime, I love taking a quick getaway from work to recharge at one of the many different places one can escape to just off the shore. I often sail to a large sandbank called Île aux Flamants, which, when the tide is low, becomes a small island. There is no cell service, and you can barely make out land on the horizon. Though it is not far, distance-wise, from the mainland, being on the sandbank feels like a true escape; there's nothing like the feeling of standing on a little strip of sand in the middle of the Indian Ocean with not a single person, car, or building as far as the eye can see.

Like most of what we do for fun in Mauritius, this is a casual outing, so all we bring is a picnic of fresh foods; swimwear; and most importantly, plenty of sunscreen. Being in the sun is wonderful, and crucial for getting enough Vitamin D. My mom taught us from a young age to take care of our skin, so I never leave home without sunscreen that is at least SPF 50. This is especially important on a beach or a sandbank, where there really is no shade. To fuel us for an active day outdoors, we focus on snacks and drinks that are nourishing, hydrating, and easy to take on the go. A light papaya salad is cooling and travels well. (The longer the papaya marinates in its juices, the better it tastes.) Steamed okra with lemon is easy finger food, and very nutritious as well. (It is full of vitamins and minerals and even has some protein.) And there are always some *gato piment*, a specialty of Mauritius and our home, which taste particularly good after an afternoon of play on the water.

Other than that, a bathing suit is all you need—though in my opinion, the more swimwear the better. There are so many different things to do in the water and on the beach that I like to bring plenty of options, and cycle through them as I go from activity to activity. Bathing suits are the one type of gear that I'm never afraid to overpack.

This page: A day at the beach doesn't have to be lazy. When we're at the sandbank, we're running, diving off boats, doing yoga, and rarely sitting down. *Following spread: Gato piment* are the official food of the Rountree family home—we are famous for them. When guests come to the house, we always have a tray ready to eat, plus plenty of the batter ready to make. These fritters of dal (served with tomato *satini* and a spicy *piment* sauce) are also a great "recovery" food that fuels us through our active beach outings.

Fresh Island Style

GATO PIMENT FRITTERS
**MAKES ABOUT 2 DOZEN FRITTERS,
ABOUT 8 SERVINGS**

2 cups yellow split peas
1 teaspoon salt
18 curry leaves
4 scallions, finely chopped
Leaves of 1 bunch cilantro, chopped
1 tablespoon cumin seeds
1 tablespoon fennel seeds
¼ cup minced fresh chives
Cold-pressed vegetable oil for frying

Wash the split peas in running water. Transfer to a large bowl with water to cover by several inches and soak for 2 to 4 hours to soften, then drain thoroughly. Add the salt to the drained split peas and in a food processor or blender, grind into a paste.

Finely chop 8 of the curry leaves. Leave the remaining 10 leaves whole. In a large bowl, mix the scallions, cilantro, cumin, and fennel into the ground split pea mixture with a wooden spoon. Mix in the chopped curry leaves and chives. Let the mixture sit at room temperature for 30 minutes to let the flavors infuse. If the mixture looks watery, blot excess water with a paper towel.

Line a baking sheet with paper towels and set aside. Fill a large pot with high sides with several inches of oil for frying. You will probably need about 2 cups. Bring the oil to temperature for deep-frying, about 350°F. Add the whole curry leaves.

Pull off a small amount of the mixture and shape into a ball the size of a golf ball. Drop into the oil. If the oil is the correct temperature, it will sizzle. Continue with the remaining mixture, regulating the temperature so the oil remains hot. Work in batches to avoid crowding the pot. As the balls become golden and crispy, remove with a slotted spoon or skimmer and place them on the prepared baking sheet to soak up the excess oil.

Let the fritters cool for 5 minutes before serving. Serve with Tomato Salsa (Tomato Satini) (see recipe on page 118) and Piment Sauce (see recipe below).

PIMENT SAUCE
MAKES ¼ CUP SAUCE

2 cups red or green chili peppers,
   stalks and seeds removed
½ teaspoon pink Himalayan salt
½ teaspoon grated lemon zest
½ teaspoon freshly squeezed lemon juice
2 cloves garlic, peeled
3½ tablespoons extra-virgin olive oil

Place all ingredients in a blender. Blend until smooth. Sauce can be stored in the refrigerator for up to 2 weeks.

THAI PAPAYA AND COCONUT SALAD
SERVES 1

½ green papaya, julienned
1 small red onion, sliced
5 to 6 cherry tomatoes, halved
1 1-inch piece ginger, peeled
   and julienned
½ cup fresh sliced coconut
1 red chili pepper, sliced
2 teaspoons light soy sauce
2 teaspoons tamarind paste
2 teaspoons freshly squeezed lime juice
1 tablespoon chopped garlic
1½ teaspoons toasted sesame seeds
2 tablespoons coarsely chopped
   roasted peanuts
3 tablespoons chopped scallion
¼ cup loosely packed cilantro leaves
¼ cup loosely packed mint leaves
Salt and freshly ground black pepper
   to taste

In a large bowl, combine the papaya, red onion, cherry tomatoes, ginger, coconut, and chili. In a small bowl whisk together the soy sauce, tamarind, lime juice, and garlic. Pour over the salad and toss to combine. Sprinkle on the sesame seeds, peanuts, scallion, cilantro, and mint. Toss and then taste and adjust seasoning.

Refrigerate covered for at least 2 hours and as long as 8 hours. Serve chilled.

Note: This recipe also works well with avocado slices instead of coconut slices.

"Sunshine is crucial
to a good mood,
and in Mauritius we're
lucky to have plenty of it.
But I'm very careful
about my exposure.
I never go out without
a hat, sunglasses, and
plenty of sunscreen,
and I try to avoid being
outside at midday."

Fresh Island Style

YOUNG OKRA SALAD
SERVES 4

1¾ pounds young okra
¼ cup extra-virgin olive oil
3 tablespoons freshly squeezed lemon juice
3 tablespoons sugarcane vinegar or apple
  cider vinegar with ¼ teaspoon turbinado sugar
1 small red chili pepper, seeds removed and cut
  into strips
1 cup loosely packed cilantro leaves
1 cup sliced red onion
Salt and freshly ground black pepper to taste

Clean the okra without opening it. Prepare a bowl of ice water and set aside. Meanwhile, bring a large pot of water to a boil. Add the okra and cook for 3 minutes. Drain and transfer to the ice water.

In a medium bowl, combine the olive oil, lemon juice, and vinegar. Whisk to combine and stir in the chili pepper. Drain the okra and transfer to a bowl. Chop the cilantro and add to the okra along with the onion. Season with salt and black pepper. Dress the okra with some of the vinegar mixture, toss, then taste and adjust. Serve immediately.

This page: When we do yoga on the beach, the sequence is more free-flowing than what you'd find in a class. We start with a few warrior poses to warm up, then work on some balancing. It is hard to stay steady on the sand, but doing these poses on the beach makes you stronger and better when you go back to hard ground. *Following spread:* My niece looks out at the old lighthouse on Île aux Fouquets (also known as Île au Phare), which is one of Mauritius's national parks.

Fresh Island Style

81

To
Market

When I return to Mauritius after being abroad, I love to stop at my favorite *marchand* (stall merchant) in the Mahébourg market for a *dholl puri*—a savory pancake made from dal—on the way from the airport. Once I've had that, I know I'm home. (I wouldn't dream of picking up any gato piment because I know a batch will be waiting for me when I get to the house.) The markets in Mauritius—almost every village has one—are fun places to experience the island's amazing edible treasures. Walk the stalls and let vendors offer you tastes of starfruit, then gaze at piles of bright green okra, tiny baby pineapples and bananas, or, on the other of end of the spectrum, avocados the size of melons.

Going into a local market or roadside stall after being at the beach can feel like a return to civilization, but the capital, Port Louis, on the north side of the island, is Mauritius at its most urban. When I was growing up, it was my connection to the rest of world. (As a child we would drive several hours to Port Louis to go to the movies, because the only theater was there.) Port Louis has elegant mosques, a thriving Chinatown, and an even larger produce market that shows off the vibrant bounty of fruits and vegetables from all over the island. It is also a great place to experience one of the things Mauritius is most famous for: cultural and religious diversity, and the unique melting pot this has created. To take just one example: my beloved dholl puri and gato piment trace their origins to Indian cuisine, but are called by Creole names, a language that is used by Mauritians of many different ethnicities.

In the markets, you see the stunning, staggering abundance of tropical produce that the island offers. Each time I go, I love being surprised by which new fruits and vegetables are in season—even now, I sometimes discover new ones—and my trips to the market give me inspiration for creating new recipes. Plus, you know that as you travel around the island, you're never far from a delicious treat.

MADAME ROSE

A variety of homemade piment and achar at a
roadside kiosk near Le Morne, in the south.

Kiosks like Madame Rose are found by the roads and in the markets all over the island and they are all delicious. No need to make a detour to find the perfect place, because you can never go wrong.

Dholl puri is a savory pancake made from yellow dal (split peas), served by *marchands* all over the island. The best are delicious plain, but they are typically served with various chutneys and piment sauce (spicy sauce; see recipe on page 69) rolled inside. In the market, you can choose which condiments you want (and also add achar, a pickled garnish used in Indian cooking) to make your *dholl puri* as spicy or piquant as you like. Here's a tip: Fresh pancakes are usually brought to the stall every half hour, so if the stack is getting low, ask the *marchand* when the new ones are coming out. If you can wait, it's worth it—the fresh ones practically melt in your mouth.

Opposite: Choose your produce wisely: The color of the skin and flesh are good hints of how fruits and vegetables will taste. For example, the darker orange the flesh is inside the *giraumon* (the large slices of pumpkin that I'm looking at), the sweeter it will be. *Above, right*: We use *pommes d'amour* (small tomatoes that are particularly juicy and sweet) to make *satini* (Creole for salsa), because the juiciness marinates the mixture, and the sweetness balances the spice. Homemade *satini* is a staple of every Mauritian kitchen.

Above, left and right: Sacks of dal, chickpea, beans, lentils, and dried chili peppers at the market in Port Louis. After I pick my vegetables, I choose a grain or a legume and spices to round out my meal. *Opposite*: There's so much wonderful produce in Mauritius that it can't be contained in the marketplace. This vendor, for instance, has her stall on a side street outside Mahébourg. Always keep your eyes open when you are walking or driving around the island because you never know what small, special treat you might find.

95

PAPAYA BREAD
MAKES 1 LARGE LOAF

Filling
1 cup raisins
¾ cup rum
2 cups julienned ripe papaya

Dough
½ teaspoon active dry or instant yeast
3 cups warm water
10½ cups bread flour
½ cup rye flour
1 teaspoon salt

At least 3 days before you plan to bake the bread, combine the raisins and rum in a small bowl or jar and macerate.

For the dough, in a small bowl, combine the yeast and ¼ cup of the water. Stir to dissolve and set aside until foamy, about 5 minutes.

In a stand mixer fitted with the paddle, combine the flours and salt. Add the water with the yeast and then the remaining water in a thin stream. Mix at low speed until it has formed a smooth dough that pulls away from the side of the bowl, about 4 to 5 minutes. (If the dough is too dry, add water in small amounts; if the dough is overly wet, add flour in small amounts.)

Transfer the dough to a large bowl or container, cover tightly, and allow to rise slowly at room temperature until doubled, 24 to 72 hours. If you reach the 72-hour mark and you are not ready to bake the bread yet, refrigerate the dough until you are ready to use it. Remove the dough from the refrigerator at least 1 hour before shaping.

Turn the dough out onto a lightly floured work surface. Pressing gently with your hands, shape it into a rectangle. Arrange the julienned papaya

in 3 rows. Sprinkle the rum-soaked raisins evenly over the surface. Roll the dough up jelly-roll style, tucking in the ends.

Transfer the bread to a pan with the seam on the bottom, cover loosely with a clean dish towel, and allow to rise at room temperature until slightly puffy, about 1 hour.

Preheat the oven to 500°F. Place the bread in the oven and immediately turn the temperature down to 425°F. Bake until loaf is brown, crust is firm, and loaf sounds hollow when tapped, about 45 minutes.

Mauritius has a very special bread culture. There is
a strong French influence on the baking tradition, so
breadmaking is quite revered. This combines with
the bounty of tropical ingredients of the island, with
results like this *miche* filled with papaya and raisin.

VEGETABLE PHO
SERVES 4

1 onion, unpeeled, halved
5 slices peeled fresh ginger
2 star anise pods
2 tablespoons soy sauce
1 tablespoon salt
4 cups dried mushroom mixture
1 12-ounce package dried rice noodles
1 pound fresh shiitake mushrooms,
    stems removed
¼ cup peanut oil
1 carrot, peeled, julienned or grated
½ cup chopped cilantro
1 tablespoon chopped scallions
1½ cups bean sprouts
Leaves of 1 bunch Thai basil
1 lime, quartered
¼ cup hoisin sauce
¼ cup chili-garlic sauce

Preheat the oven to 425°F. Place the onion on a baking sheet and roast in the preheated oven until blackened and soft, about 45 minutes. Set aside to cool.

Place the onion, ginger, star anise, soy sauce, and salt in a large stockpot. Add 4 quarts of water. Bring to a boil and reduce heat to low. Add dried mushrooms and simmer over low heat until mushrooms are very soft and broth is fragrant and flavorful, at least 6 and up to 10 hours. Strain the broth into a saucepan and set aside.

Place rice noodles in large bowl filled with room temperature water and soak for 1 hour.

Slice the fresh mushrooms. Heat the peanut oil in a large skillet. Add the mushrooms and cook, stirring occasionally, until tender, 8 to 10 minutes. Set aside.

Bring a large pot of water to a boil and after the noodles have soaked, place them in the boiling water for 1 minute. Remove and drain. Bring stock to a simmer.

Divide the noodles among 4 serving bowls; top with carrot, sautéed shiitake mushrooms, cilantro, and scallion. Pour hot broth over the top. Stir to combine, then let the soup sit for 1 to 2 minutes. Serve with bean sprouts, Thai basil leaves, lime wedges, hoisin sauce, and chili-garlic sauce on the side.

Fruit gets a bad rap sometimes because of its natural sugar, but it is an essential part of my diet. Fruits have many important vitamins and minerals that strengthen your immune system, so I eat them daily rather than take supplements. Because your body digests fruit quickly, it is best to have it first thing in the morning, and enjoy as many different types as possible—I try to "eat the rainbow" every day.

Lunch
from the
Garden

What I eat for lunch when I am at home is pretty simple: I look at the garden, see what looks ripe, and pick it. Freshly picked fruits and vegetables give you the maximum amount of nutrients—the more recent the produce has been harvested, the more potent the health benefits. In Mauritius, we have tropical varieties of well-known vegetables, such as *giraumon* (a large pumpkin-like gourd, like Cinderella's carriage), *margoze* (bitter melon), *chou chou* (chayote), as well as carrots, okra, eggplant, and avocados. We also grow herbs and roots like turmeric and ginger, which are tasty and have healthy medicinal properties. (Turmeric is frequently used in Indian cooking, which has many influences on Mauritian cuisine.) To turn this into a meal, I round out whatever vegetables and spices I'm using with dal, chickpeas, another legume, or a grain. It's basically a "build-your-own-bowl" experience every day, and I try to use that principle to create meals wherever I go. No matter what meal it is, you can never go wrong with a combination of good produce, flavorful spices, filling grains or legumes, and a nourishing fat, like avocado.

On days when family comes around for lunch, if there's time afterwards, we sit on the veranda playing cards, board games, or solitaire on a wood board. We always have some traditional Mauritian snacks on hand (roasted peanuts and peas, banana chips, and my beloved Twisties) in case we get peckish, as well as water steeped with lemon and herbs. The lemon in the water helps alkalize the body, which is particularly important in a tropical climate. In Mauritius, it is easy to get completely absorbed in one's computer—it is the tie to the rest of the world—so it's nice to take some time to enjoy one another's company without our devices, and the pause from our devices is great for overall well-being.

It is very energizing to fuel oneself with fresh produce. My favorite things to eat are homegrown fruit and vegetables, but when I travel, I look to whatever is at its peak and try to build my meals from the purest ingredients available.

"Cook with fresh
and local ingredients
whenever you can,
but don't stress about
being perfect all of the
time. It is also important
to listen to your
body, and give it
what it wants."

This page: Looking after a garden is rewarding because your care turns a seed into something that nourishes your friends and family. But you don't need acres and acres—a small herb garden on a windowsill or a single tomato plant can provide the same joy and tastiness to the food you cook. *Following spread*: We sometime use large palm leaves like these as table runners to add a tropical touch to a meal.

We use latanier palm leaves, or sometimes
banana leaves (*opposite*), to wrap up
bundles of produce, such as on page 30.
Above: A stalk of soon-to-be-ripe bananas.

MOONG DAL
SERVES 6

2½ cups moong dal (dried mung beans)
1 teaspoon salt
1 cup diced fresh tomatoes
Freshly squeezed juice of ½ lemon
2 teaspoons grated ginger
½ teaspoon ground turmeric
1 tablespoon vegetable oil
1 teaspoon cumin seeds
¼ teaspoon minced dried red chili pepper
2 cloves garlic, minced
1 pinch asafoetida powder
½ cup chopped cilantro

Place the dal in a strainer, rinse until water runs clear, and pick through to check for any stones. Transfer to a medium saucepan and pour in 2½ cups water. Cover with a lid and let the dal soak for at least 30 minutes and up to 1 hour.

Stir the salt into the beans. Bring to a boil over medium heat. Reduce to medium-low and cook until dal dissolves into a thick, soupy mixture, about 15 minutes. The mixture should be the consistency of porridge. If it seems too dry, add water in small amounts. Stir in the tomatoes, lemon juice, grated ginger, and turmeric.

In a small skillet, heat the oil. Add the cumin seeds and the minced dried chili pepper and cook, stirring frequently, until they give off a strong fragrance. Add the garlic and asafoetida and stir briskly to keep the garlic from burning, then stir the mixture into the beans. Sprinkle on the cilantro, stir to combine, and serve hot or warm.

GREEN SOUP
(BOUILLON WITH WATERCRESS)
SERVES 4

2 cloves garlic, peeled, crushed and chopped
1 teaspoon grated ginger
Salt to taste
1 large bunch watercress or bok choy, trimmed

Place 5 cups water in a large soup pot or stockpot and bring to a boil. Add the garlic, ginger, and salt. Boil for 1 minute, then add the watercress or bok choy and cook for 5 minutes. Let the soup sit off the heat for another 5 minutes before serving.

Fresh Island Style

117

SQUASH FRICASSÉE
SERVES 4

1 medium winter squash, about 1 pound
2 teaspoons cold-pressed vegetable oil
1 small onion, peeled and minced
2 cloves garlic, peeled and minced
¼ teaspoon grated ginger
1 sprig thyme
1 sprig parsley
Salt to taste
Freshly ground black pepper to taste

Peel and seed the squash. Cut the flesh into a large dice. You should have 4 to 5 cups. Heat the oil in a large saucepan and add the onion. Cook until soft, about 3 minutes, then add the garlic and ginger and cook for 3 additional minutes. Add the squash, thyme sprig, parsley sprig, salt, and pepper. Cover and cook over medium heat until squash is soft, about 10 minutes. If the pumpkin starts to stick to the bottom of the pan, sprinkle a small amount of water on top.

Remove and discard thyme and parsley sprigs. Mash the pumpkin in the pot. It should be thick. If it is too watery, cook uncovered for 5 additional minutes. Serve immediately.

TOMATO SALSA (TOMATO SATINI)
MAKES ABOUT 2 CUPS SALSA

4 medium tomatoes
Leaves of 5 sprigs cilantro
2 scallions
3 chives
Salt to taste

Chop the tomatoes, cilantro, scallions, and chives and combine in a bowl. Stir in the salt.

Note: You can also make salsa with green mango or cucumber in place of the tomatoes.

EINKORN BREAD
MAKES 1 LOAF

1¼ cups warm water

1½ teaspoons active dry or instant yeast

2 tablespoons extra-virgin olive oil
  or melted and cooled unsalted butter

1 tablespoon sugar or honey

3¾ cups Einkorn flour

1¼ teaspoons salt

1 cup mixed seeds, such as sesame,
  flax, and chia

Butter and/or extra-virgin olive oil
  for loaf pan and wax paper

In a large bowl, combine warm water, yeast, oil or butter, and sugar or honey. Stir until creamy.

Sprinkle the flour over the yeast mixture. Sprinkle the salt on top. Mix with a spatula, working from the bottom of the bowl to the top, until the flour is absorbed and you have a wet, sticky dough. Add the seeds to the dough and mix well. Cover tightly with wax paper and let rise for 45 minutes.

Preheat the oven to 375°F and butter an 8½ x 4½-inch loaf pan. Transfer the dough to a lightly floured work surface. The dough will feel very sticky and wet, but add as little flour as possible. Use a bench scraper to handle it if needed. Shape the dough into a loaf. Sprinkle some seeds over the top of the loaf.

Place the dough in the loaf pan seam side down and cover loosely with buttered or oiled wax paper. Let rise for 30 minutes. Remove the wax paper and bake in the preheated oven until crust is brown and firm, about 40 minutes. Cool completely before slicing.

The variety of tropical flora in Mauritius is incredible—with all of the colors and textures here, it is impossible to have a dull arrangement. The orange and red spiky flowers in the arrangement on the Ping-Pong table (*opposite*) are bird-of-paradise; the white and pink flowers that are slim like candles are called *fleurs la bougie*. The flowers that I'm holding (*this page, right*) are called heliconia, or lobster claws. The feathers (*this page, top right*) we've picked up over the years from our lovely macaw. *Following spread*: The exterior and veranda of the house I grew up in.

Fresh Island Style

123

The afternoon sun in Mauritius is intense, so we always follow lunch with more hydration. Lemon water is great for protecting the immune system and alkalizing the body; it's also very nourishing at a cellular level. Adding mint or other fresh herbs to the water makes it taste even more refreshing.

This page and following spread: My family and traditional Mauritian snacks are the things I miss most when I am away from the island. Roasted peanuts and peas, dried banana chips, and various treats made from *gram*, a chickpea flour, are sold in markets and stalls all over Mauritius.

129

Recharge *on the* Rocks

Around midday, when the heat and humidity start to get intense, it is tempting to look to sweets and caffeine for energy, or wish for a nap. But the effects of sugar and coffee are harsh and unstable, and within our busy, chaotic lives, it is nearly impossible to rest in the afternoon. So instead, I like to fight daytime fatigue with two weapons: water and a walk.

Cold water is nature's wonder drug; in addition to water's naturally invigorating properties, being in fresh, cool water has a number of other health benefits, such as improving circulation, reducing muscular inflammation, and boosting metabolism. When I feel myself start to fade, my favorite way to perk myself back up is going for a swim in the fresh water pool near our house. But you don't need to completely immerse yourself in the water to experience its energizing benefits. When I'm not at home, running my wrists under cool water for a few minutes has the same renewing effect.

Taking a walk is another trick I use when I need to recharge. Even when it is hot, I find that spending a little time in nature helps revive me. (Though I try to stay in the shade, or wait until it's a little overcast at the beach, to avoid the depleting effects of the sun.) Experiencing the colors of the flowers, the sounds of the ocean, and the feeling of my feet sinking into the sand cuts through any brain fog I have. Mauritius is a volcanic island, so if you are out on the rocks, you can absorb some of the volcanic energy too. (There is also an energy vortex on the island, which people visit to align their chakras.) But every landscape has its own invigorating qualities. So wherever you are, taking a little bit of time to walk outdoors (barefoot, ideally on the grass or in the sand) will help you re-center and maintain sharp focus for the rest of the day. I particularly love exploring the beach with my young niece, Kiera—the change of perspective you get from being with a child helps awaken the senses because you see everything from a different, purer point of view.

Opposite: A burst of color from brightly colored flowers is visually invigorating and a natural mood enhancer. Here we've woven *fleurs la bougie* (the Creole name for this island flower) through a wicker towel basket to add a refreshing pop of tropical color poolside. *Above right*: Whether it is a dip in a pool, an outdoor waterfall shower, or simply running your hands under a faucet for a few seconds, a jolt of cold water is a great way to recharge—it's the best natural pick-me-up.

Fresh Island Style

141

You don't need much for an impromptu stroll on the beach, but it's always good to be prepared with a few essentials: a simple cotton blanket or tablecloth; easy, shareable snacks like fresh fruit or a baguette; and, of course, plenty of water and sunscreen. In Mauritius, we carry everything to the beach in sturdy straw *paniers*.

Opposite: One of nature's great powers is its ability to awaken the senses. Walking on the beach, in particular, can be a complete sensory immersion: there are the sounds of crashing waves, the dramatic contrast between the water and volcanic rocks, and feeling the texture of the sand between your toes.

143

"Keeping yourself energized and positive during the day is crucial to overall well-being. When I feel myself fading, a few minutes of invigorating activity instantly refreshes me, and makes me feel ready for whatever the rest of the day brings."

Fresh Island Style

147

Quiet
Time

On a tropical island, where the heat and sun get more intense as the day goes on—or alternatively, a powerful thunderstorm builds to a downpour—afternoons offer a natural pause. And I find that my energy, creativity, and well-being benefit from an afternoon check-in with myself.

Meditation is a crucial part of this; for me, it is vital for focus and productivity. If I skimp on my meditation practice, I feel the difference in what I accomplish during the day. I practice Transcendental Meditation (TM), for twenty minutes twice a day. That might sound like a lot of time, but it pays back in how it enhances the quality of what you do, and how you deal with people and difficult situations. That said, as with yoga, even taking two minutes during the day to concentrate on your breath can be extremely beneficial for energy and stress relief. Meditation is about creating inward focus, not emptying your head, so don't worry if your mind wanders—that's a natural part of meditating, and all you need to do is bring yourself back to your breath to return to a meditative state.

I find that my mind is the most open to ideas and inspiration after a few minutes of re-centering, so after I've meditated, I try to do something creative, such as sketching new patterns for my swimwear line. I never plan in advance what I'm going to paint, because when I'm in this centered frame of mind, I find that inspiration flows through me.

Mindfulness is equally important when it comes to eating, at any time of day. The best part about this is that it is not expensive or complicated to develop a mindful approach to eating. In general, I try to eat the best quality of food as possible (pure dark chocolate as opposed to candy bars; homecooked treats instead of packaged ones), but I never think of food as "good" or "bad." The stress and guilt people feel about food can contribute to weight gain; if you instead choose foods consciously, trying to eat for fuel and taste rather than on autopilot you will enjoy everything you eat more and be healthier at the same time.

I often have a tisane in the afternoon, which is simply water boiled with herbs or roots such as lemongrass, ginger, and turmeric. I'll also add a few cracks of black pepper to help activate the nutrients of the herbs, and enhance the warming effect. Tisanes are great to have after a meal because they aid digestion, and they have anti-inflammatory properties as well. Because they are not caffeinated, they can steep for as long as you like (and you can continue to add hot water). You can also refrigerate the tea and drink it warm or cold the next day.

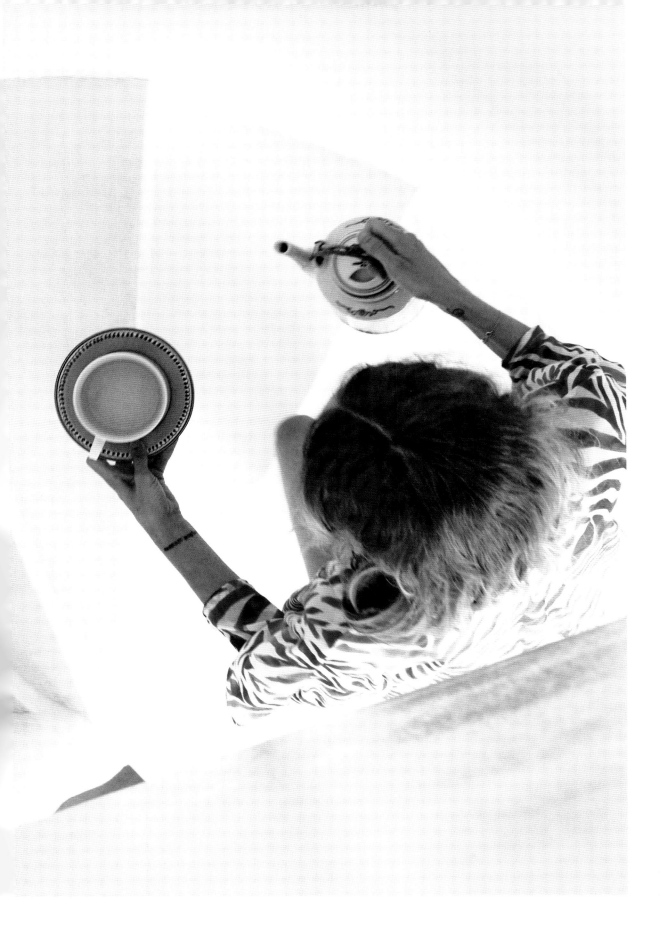

153

This page: Quiet time doesn't mean idle time; I'm most creative after I've taken time to re-center. This is when I love to work on prints for my swimwear line. *Opposite*: This painting is by my great-uncle Frank Avray Wilson, an early Abstract Expressionistist in Paris and London. The ceramics are by Paul Jackson.

BANANA TART

MAKES ONE 9-INCH TART,
APPROXIMATELY 8 SERVINGS

25 very ripe bananas
2 vanilla beans
One 9-inch pre-made tart shell,
  homemade or store-bought
Crème anglaise for serving (optional)

Peel and roughly chop the bananas and place in a large saucepan. Slice the vanilla beans lengthwise and scrape the seeds into the pot, then add the beans.

Stir well to combine and cook over low heat, stirring occasionally, for 8 hours. The bananas will give off a lot of liquid. Eventually the liquid will evaporate and the bananas will reduce significantly, leaving you with a smooth brown paste.

When the banana mixture is very dense, allow it to cool, then spread evenly in the tart shell that has been pre-baked for 15 to 20 minutes in a 300°F oven. Bake the tart filled with the banana mixture for 20 to 30 minutes, until the crust is golden brown. Top with crème anglaise, if using, just before serving.

Fresh Island Style

Opposite: There is great beauty in small
things. A single blossom in a glass, a colorful
feather in a vase, or a plain white shell on a
bedside table is often even more evocative
of joy than an elaborate piece of decor.

159

NONNA LIZZY'S OATCAKES
MAKES 12 TO 15 OATCAKES

½ cup chopped walnuts
½ cup chopped almonds
5 cups rolled oats
1 stick (8 tablespoons) salted butter,
    melted and cooled
½ teaspoon ground cinnamon
½ cup dried cranberries
2 large eggs, lightly beaten

Preheat oven to 350°F. Spread the walnuts and almonds on a baking sheet and toast until golden and fragrant, 15 to 20 minutes. Line a second baking sheet with parchment paper and set aside.

While the nuts are toasting, mix the oats with the butter and cinnamon and set aside. Remove the nuts from the oven, cool briefly, then add the nuts and cranberries to the oat and butter mixture and mix well to combine. Finally, mix in the eggs.

Using your hands or an ice cream scoop, make 12 to 15 round balls of the mixture, approximately 3 inches wide, and place on the prepared baking sheet. Bake in the preheated oven until golden brown (and your kitchen smells good!), about 20 minutes. Let the oatcakes cool on the pan on a rack for 30 minutes before serving.

Pages 160-161: My mother's oatcakes are beloved by everyone in our family from the adults down to my niece, Kiera. They are simple and nourishing, so my mother makes a batch almost daily, and sends a tin over for Kiera's lunch. When the tin comes back in the afternoon, it's always empty. *This page*: The circular table stacked with books in the entryway of our home. This is the hub of the house, connecting the kitchen, dining area, porch, and bedrooms, so we often pick up books as we pass from room to room. It is also one of the favorite napping spots of our dog, Teddy.

163

REFRESHING DRINKS

SERVES 1

The food we eat affects how we feel, think, and act. Every day comes with a different challenge to overcome. So whether you're tired, crazed, stressed, scattered, or just need a pick-me-up, these juices will make you feel good. They ground, center, and revitalize.

If using a juicer, wash all fruits and vegetables thoroughly and then press ingredients through a juicer.

You can also make these juices in a blender. Wash all fruits and vegetables thoroughly. Cut the fruits and vegetables into small chunks and place the ingredients in the blender with ¾ cup water. Blend on high until combined. If the consistency is too thick, add water in small amounts, blending between additions until the mixture is a slurry. Place a fine mesh strainer over a tall glass. Transfer the contents of the blender into the strainer and press firmly on the solids to extract as much liquid as possible. Drink immediately for maximum vitamin strength.

Leftover juice can be stored in an airtight container in the refrigerator for up to 3 days.

APPLE CLEANSER

2 apples, halved and cored
1 pinch ground cayenne
1 tablespoon maple syrup

GLOW GREEN

2 Granny Smith apples, halved and cored
3 leaves kale, ribs removed
Freshly squeezed juice of ½ lemon
1 cup tightly packed spinach leaves

RAINBOW CHASER

1 apple, halved and cored
3 medium carrots, peeled
2 medium celery ribs
½ grapefruit, peeled, pith removed, and seeded
1 orange, peeled, pith removed, and seeded

RESTART RED

1 apple, halved and cored
1 medium beet, peeled
3 medium carrots, peeled
Freshly squeezed juice of ½ lemon
1 small piece fresh ginger, peeled

SUPER YELLOW

1 pinch ground cayenne
Freshly squeezed juice of ½ lemon
1 pear, halved and cored
½ pineapple spear

WATERMELON REFRESHER

2 cups peeled, seeded watermelon cubes
Freshly squeezed juice of ½ lime

SUGARCANE & LEMONGRASS DRINK

If we want an afternoon drink that is refreshing, but still soothing, we have a glass of lemongrass water (or a chilled tisane). To make it, boil a few stalks of lemongrass and some sliced ginger until the water becomes the color of Chardonnay. Then chill for several hours, and strain into a pitcher before serving. Lemongrass water is delicious plain, but Mauritians often serve it with raw sugarcane syrup on the side, so you can sweeten to taste. (If you can't find sugarcane syrup, agave is a good substitute.) Using a stalk of lemongrass as a stirrer is a nice touch.

Though I practice TM daily, I also love sound meditation.
Sound meditation is a type of meditation in which you are
surrounded by bowls of different sizes, which are struck
in various ways to produce deep, audible vibrations. The
heavy tones of the vibrations pull you into a different realm of
consciousness, resulting in a profound feeling of relaxation,
peace, and well-being. Experiencing the vibrations in person
is ideal, but you can also do it on your own by downloading
sound-bath recordings.

"Taking time for yourself
is essential for well-being.
Committing to brief
daily rituals of self-care
does wonders for
your mood, productivity,
and creativity. The benefits
you can reap from
just a few minutes of inward
focus are astonishing."

Sunset
Dinner

There are many amazing things about life in Mauritius—the natural beauty, proximity to the sea, tropical weather. But those of us who call the island home experience the same quotidian occurrences there as everywhere else. It can be tricky, for instance, to get a group of friends together, though some of our logistical challenges are particular to island living. I'm based in the south, and most of my friends live in the north, which is at least an hour away on the single two-lane road that rings the island. When we do get together, our focus is on spending time with one another. We keep everything else—the food and drink, the table setting, the dress code—casual and stress-free.

For food, we like to do a mix of healthy finger food (summer rolls and toasts topped with spreads and raw vegetables), with some traditional Mauritian dishes (a curry or a vegetable biryani), of course. For drinks, there is no need for a fancy cocktail—a bottle of rosé against the sunset is the perfect complement to any outdoor meal.

Often we gather around a simple table on the veranda or on the beach, and our entertainment is simply catching up with one another. But if we want to partake of something more festive, we'll listen to live sega music and watch the dancing. You can see sega dancing all over the island, in different kinds of settings, from formal choreographed performances put on by hotels to casual gatherings in the street or on the beach. Sega can be done with a large group of trained dancers, but it can also be done by smaller groups, or even a single person. Songs are sung in Creole, accompanied by guitar, triangle, and the *ravanne* (which is like a tambourine). Sega is exemplary of the Mauritian way of life—colorful, full of joy, and inclusive. It is a very carefree dance, and it's all in the hips—hence why the women always wear cropped tops—and the music is intoxicatingly upbeat. Sega is about being happy and spreading that joy to others, a feeling that is at once quintessentially Mauritian and a powerful reminder to enjoy the company around you.

"The most important part about getting together with friends should be enjoying each other. No matter where I am in the world, I keep my gatherings casual, communal, and unfussy. I focus my energy on the company, and don't stress about the planning."

This page: More evidence that once I'm in Mauritius, it's hard to get me out of a bikini! One of my favorite evening looks is throwing a colorful sarong over my swimsuit, or putting one of my short kimonos over shorts, as my friend Laetitia (third from left) has done.

177

Ever since I was a child, I've loved sega dancing and the flowy, colorful outfits the dancers wear. The dance is all in the hips and the costume accentuates that—the dancers fan their skirts out, and their tops are cropped to show off their midriffs. I also love how sega embraces the outdoors— even when it is performed on stage, you usually watch it outside in the tropical air. And everyone is welcome to join in, so it is symbolic of the inclusiveness of our island.

181

Opposite: Hollowed-out coconut shells can be used either as serving dishes or as individual bowls for friends. *This page*: When guests arrive, I like to serve a selection of miniature avocado toasts (see page 31), topped with whatever greens and vegetables I have on hand, instead of an egg.

RAW SPRING ROLLS WITH TAMARI-GINGER DIPPING SAUCE
MAKES 12 ROLLS

12 round rice paper wrappers,
8½ inches in diameter
6 large Romaine or butter lettuce leaves,
torn in half
2 carrots, peeled and julienned
½ cucumber, julienned
⅓ cup chopped purple cabbage
1¼ ounces vermicelli rice noodles,
soaked in hot water and drained
Leaves of 1 bunch fresh mint
2 tablespoons sesame seeds
Sea salt to taste
¼ cup tamari
1 1-inch piece ginger, peeled
and finely grated

Lightly moisten the surface of a cutting board. Fill a large shallow bowl with lukewarm water. Submerge a rice paper wrapper in the warm water until pliable, 10 to 15 seconds. Transfer the wrapper to the moistened cutting board.

Arrange a lettuce leaf half horizontally on the rice paper near the bottom but leaving a ½-inch to 1-inch margin free. Place some of the julienned carrots and cucumber on top of the lettuce, arranging them in the same direction as the rib of the leaf. Place cabbage on top. Add a small amount of the vermicelli, and scatter on some mint leaves.

Fold the sides of the wrapper over the ingredients. Starting from the bottom, roll away from you, keeping the roll tight. Place seam side down on a serving platter. Repeat with remaining wrappers and ingredients, keeping the rolls in a single layer.

Toast the sesame seeds lightly in a small frying pan with a pinch of sea salt. Sprinkle over the spring rolls. In a small bowl, whisk together the tamari and ginger. Serve spring rolls immediately with tamari-ginger sauce for dipping on the side.

VEGETABLE BIRYANI
SERVES 4

2 tablespoons vegetable oil
2 medium yellow onions, halved,
  peeled, and thinly sliced
2 medium potatoes, peeled
  and thinly sliced
2 medium carrots, peeled and diced
1 cup cauliflower florets
2 tablespoons peeled and minced garlic
2 tablespoons peeled and minced ginger
½ cup plain yogurt
2 to 3 tablespoons Biryani Spice Mix
  (see below)
2 to 4 slices fresh green chili
Salt and freshly ground pepper to taste
1⅓ cups basmati rice
¼ teaspoon saffron
½ cup chopped cilantro
½ cup chopped fresh mint leaves
Mango chutney for serving
Raita for serving

Heat a skillet over medium-low heat. Add the oil and when it is hot add the onions. Cook the onions, stirring frequently, until deep brown and caramelized, about 20 minutes.

Combine the potatoes, carrots, and cauliflower with the garlic, ginger, yogurt, spice mix, cooked onions, and green chili. Season with salt and pepper and allow to rest at room temperature for at least 1 hour.

Meanwhile, rinse the rice and drain it. Soak the rice in cold water for 30 minutes and drain it again. In a large pot bring a generous amount of water to a boil and cook lightly. Add the rice and cook, stirring frequently, until it is about halfway cooked, about 4 minutes. It should be soft on the outside, but still brittle in the center. Drain and allow to cool.

In a stockpot with a tight-fitting lid, make a layer of about half of the vegetable mixture. Top with a layer of about half of the partially cooked rice. Make another layer of the remaining vegetable mixture and top with the remaining rice. In a small bowl, dissolve the saffron in 2½ cups water. Drizzle this mixture over the top of the rice.

Cover the pot and cook over low heat until vegetables are soft and easily pierced with a knife and rice is tender, 15 to 30 minutes. Sprinkle cilantro and mint over rice before serving. Serve with mango chutney and raita on the side.

BIRYANI SPICE MIX
MAKES ABOUT ¾ CUP SPICE MIX

1 tablespoon toasted coriander seeds
1 tablespoon toasted cumin seeds
1 1-inch piece fresh turmeric root, peeled
1½ teaspoons chili powder
½ teaspoon freshly grated nutmeg
⅓ cup cashews
1 clove garlic, peeled
1 1-inch piece ginger
¼ cup loosely packed cilantro leaves
½ cup loosely packed mint leaves

Combine all the ingredients in a blender and puree. While continuing to blend, add water in a thin stream to form a thick paste. You will need about ¼ cup water, but the amount can vary widely, so add the water gradually.

189

Having a carefree gathering means going with the flow—literally, when your table is on the beach. The tide coming in is nature telling us that it's time to bring things inside. No matter how much we're enjoying ourselves, we welcome the call—because another full day of activity starts at sunrise.

191

Recipe Index

Page number in *italics* indicate illustrations

Mauritius Addresses

ACTIVITIES / DISCOVERIES

Bois Cheri Tea Plantation and Museum
(nice views and tea tasting)
Société Usinière de Bois Cheri
Bois Cheri Road, Bois Cheri
www.saintaubin.mu
Tel. (230) 617-9109

Catamaran Cruises (catamaran day trip)
Coastal Road, Pointe d'Esny
www.catamarancruisesmauritius.com
Tel. (230) 5728-3030

Domaine des Aubineaux
(museum and manor house)
Royal Road, Forest Side, Curepipe
www.saintaubinloisirs.com
Tel. (230) 676-3089

Energy Vortex of Riambel
(meditation center and recharge)
Riambel
www.vortexriambel.com
Tel. (230) 5736-9038

Ganga Talao (Hindu sacred lake
with temples and statues)
Grand Bassin Road, Savanne

Île aux Flamants (island sandbank
in the middle of the ocean)

Île Plate (small island nature reserve)

Kayak at Île d'Ambre
(active and beautiful)
www.yemayaadventures.com
Tel. (230) 5752-0046

Kite Surfing (picturesque kite surf spot)
Le Morne

L'Aventure du Sucre
(sugarcane discovery)
Beau Plan, Pamplemousses
www.aventuredusucre.com
Tel. (230) 243-7900

La Vanille Nature Reserve
(great for families)
Senneville, Riviere des Anguilles, 60602
www.lavanille-naturepark.com
Tel. (230) 626-2503

Le Souffleur
(wild south part of the island)
Le Souffleur Access Road,
Grand Port

Pointe d'Esny and Blue Bay
(amazing crystal-clear water)

Sail with Jean Claude Farla
(authentic pirogue outing)
Tel. (230) 5423-1322

Seaplane flight tour
(see the "underwater waterfall"
from above)
Lagoon Flight
Le Morne
www.lagoonflight.com
Tel. (230) 59752424

Vitamin Sea (swim with dolphins
and whales/underwater and aerial
photoshoots)
Boat leaves from Tamarin
www.vitaminsealtd.com
Tel. (230) 5490-1450

A great website to get information
for the best adventures and places
to visit is Mauritius Explored
www.mauritiusexplored.com
info@mauritiusexplored.com

BEACHES

Gris Gris (South/wild)

La Cuvette (North/hidden away)
Riviere de Rempart, Grand Baie

Palmar (East/quiet)

Tamarin (West/surfer spot)

HIKING / WATERFALLS

Black River Gorges (day hike/picnic)
Plaine Champagne Road

Chamarel Waterfall
(272-foot waterfall/easy access)
Chamarel

Eau Bleue (secret blue waterfall)
Cluny (off Sugar Cane Road)

Ebony Forest Reserve
(indigenous forest reserve)
7 Colored Earth Road, Chamarel, 90409
www.ebonyforest.com
Tel. (230) 5865-5383

Île Aux Aigrettes (nature reserve)
Old Sands Jetty at Pointe Jerome
Tel. (230) 631-2396

La Vallee de Ferney
(beautiful forest trails to hike)
Vieux Grand Port
www.lavalleedeferney.com
Tel. (230) 634-044

Le Morne Mountain
(epic views/difficult hike)

Le Pouce Mountain
(short easy hike)

Les 7 Cascades
(hike to beautiful waterfalls)
Pitois Road, Vacoas-Phoenix

Montagne Du Lion
(best done at sunrise)

Rochester Falls
(unusual rock formations)
Pont Bon Dieu, Salazie, Flacq

Trou Aux Cerfs (dormant volcanic crater)
Trou aux Cerfs Road, Curepipe

HORSE RIDING

Centre Equestre de Riambel
(sunset ride)
Riambel
www.centreequestrederiambel.com
Tel. (230) 5729-4572

Equitation Eco-green
(riding in the water)
Haras de Morne, Le Morne
www.haras-du-morne.business.site
Tel. (230) 450-4142

HOTELS / LODGES

Constance Prince Maurice (romantic)
Choisy Road Poste De Flacq, Maurice
www.constancehotels.com
Tel. (230) 402-3636

Four Seasons Resort in Anahita
(classic/couples retreat)
Coastal Road, Beau Champ
www.fourseasons.com
Tel. (230) 402-3100

Héritage Le Telfair Golf & Wellness
Resort (chic/peaceful)
Coastal Road, Bel Ombre
www.heritageresorts.mu
Tel. (230) 601-5500

Île des Deux Cocos
(private island villa getaway)
Île des Deux Cocos, Blue Bay
www.iledesdeuxcocos.com
Tel. (230) 698-9800

La Pirogue (family/authentic)
Wolmar, Flic en Flac
www.lapirogue.com
Tel. (230) 403-3900

La Vielle Cheminée
(eco-lodge/farm)
Main Road, 90403 Chamarel
www.lavieillecheminee.com
Tel. (230) 483-4249

Le Touessrok Shangri-La
(hip/sophisticated)
Coastal Road, Trou d'Eau Douce
www.shangri-la.com
Tel. (230) 402-7400

Lux* Belle Mare (stylish)
Quatre Cocos
www.luxresorts.com
Tel. (230) 402-2000

Lux* Grand Gaube (elegant)
Coastal Road, Grand Gaube, 30617
www.luxresorts.com
Tel. (230) 204-9191

Lux* Le Morne (amazing sunset/vibe)
Coastal Road, Le Morne
www.luxresorts.com
Tel. (230) 401-4000

One & Only Le Saint Geran
(high end / classy)
Pointe de Flacq, Poste de Flacq, 41518
www.oneandonlyresorts.com
Tel. (230) 401-1688

Otentic Eco Tent (eco-lodge)
Coastal Road, Deux Frères, Grand River
South East
www.otentic.mu
Tel. (230) 5 941-4888

Preskil Island Resort (family)
Pointe Jerome, Mahébourg, Maurice
www.southerncrosshotels.mu
Tel. (230) 604-1000

Salt of Palmar (sustainable/local)
Quatre Cocos
www.saltresorts.com
Tel. (230) 401-8500

Shanti Maurice Resort & Spa
(ayurvedic/relaxing)
Coastal Road, Saint Felix
www.shantimaurice.com
Tel. (230) 603-7200

20 Degrés Sud—Relais & Château
(intimate/charming)
Coastal Road Pointe Malartic Mauritius,
Grand Baie
www.20degressud.com
Tel. (230) 263-5000

MARKETS

Central Market
9 Corderie Street, Port Louis

Flacq Market
Central Flacq

Mahébourg Market
Rue de la Passe, Mahébourg

Quatre Bornes Market Fair
St Jean Road, Quatre Bornes

RESTAURANTS

Blue Marlin Restaurant at the Paradis
Beachcomber Hotel (beach views)
Le Morne Penninsula
www.beachcomber-hotels.com

Chez Rosy (local Creole seafood)
Gris Gris, Souillac
Tel. (230) 625-4179

Eat with Fingers (organic, raw, vegan)
Vingt Pieds Road, Grand Baie
www.eatwithfingers.com
Tel. (230) 5813-5449

La Case du Pecheur
(fresh fish, mangrove views)
Royal Road, Bamboo Virieux,
Vieux Grand Port
Tel. (230) 634-5675

La Cosa Nostra
(wood-oven Italian pizza)
Corner Anthurium Lane, Royal Road,
Tamarin, 90921
Tel. (230) 483-6169

La Table du Château (fine dining)
Domaine de Labourdonnais, Mapou
www.tableduchateau.com
Tel. (230) 266-7172

Le Bois Cheri
(located within a tea plantation)
Société Usinière de Bois Cheri,
Bois Cheri, Grand Bois
www.saintaubin.mu
Tel. (230) 5471-1216

Le Whatever (French/great wines)
La Place Cap, Tamarin, 90901
www.lewhatever.mu
Tel. (230) 483-7810

Maison Eureka
(Creole cuisine/restored colonial house)
Eureka Lane, Montagne Ory, Moka
www.eureka-house.com
Tel. (230) 433-8477

Moustache Bistro
(French bistro/dinner only)
Royal Road, La Mivoie, Tamarin
Tel. (230) 483-7728

Rum Shack (local food/great setting)
Shanti Maurice Hotel
Coastal Road, Saint Felix
Tel. (230) 603-7200

Varangue Sur Morne
(incredible ocean views)
110, Plaine Champagne Road, Chamarel
Tel. (230) 483-6610

Page 196: View of Le Morne Mountain
with the "underwater waterfall" nearby.
Page 198: Traditional pirogues in
Mahébourg.
Page 199: An ice cream truck at the
Mahébourg waterfront.
Page 201: The beach at Lux* Grand
Gaube hotel.
Pages 202–203: Sega Dancers on the
beach in Palmar.
Page 204: Alicia and Sveva at Pointe
D'Esny.
Pages 206–207: View of Lion Mountain
from the ocean.
Page 208: Alicia at La Prairie Beach.

Acknowledgments

It has always been my dream to write a book about Mauritius—for years I visualized it in my mind. To have it become a reality has been quite extraordinary, and I'm so grateful to everyone who helped make my dream into the book you are holding.

Sandy Gilbert, my non-stop superwoman of an editor, tirelessly guided me through the entire process. Thank you as well to Charles Miers, the publisher of Rizzoli, for giving me the chance to share my vision of Mauritius.

Caitlin Leffel, stepped into my world, and helped me voice the story I've always wanted to share about my home.

Dewey Nicks brought the enthusiasm, vision, and style I dreamed of to the pictures he created for this book.

Shawn Merz was our secret weapon—he provided invaluable creative ideas and endless energy for getting things done, always with a smile.

James Michael Butterfield kept me looking fresh through long, hot days of shooting, and kept us all amused by his unfortunate encounters with coral and mosquitos.

Charlotte Heal, created the modern yet colorful design of this book, with beautiful details and a timeless feel.

This book may never have happened had Glenda Bailey not given me the chance to introduce her readers to my Mauritius in the pages of *Harper's Bazaar*. Thank you for the opportunity to tell my story, and for the beautiful foreword.

It was wonderful to work with so many local companies in the creation of this book. In particular, I'd like to thank Andreas Habermeyer of Identical Pictures; Virginie Dalais at Euphoria; Yuni Furniture & Lifestyle; Anne Bedel; Paul Jones and the entire staff of the Lux* Resorts & Hotels.

To the people who have worked with my family for many years—Nancy, Pascaline, Jessica, and Manoj—thank you for being a part of this book, and helping us with whatever we needed.

Thanks to Spring Studios for generously supporting the project.

Finally, I want to thank my family, not only for encouraging my dream of making a book, but also for being such an important part of its creation. My mother, Elizabeth, is my rock and was always there with a helping hand. My sister Harriet and niece Sveva gamely interrupted their holiday to appear in the book whenever I needed them. My brother Teig and his wife Marine let me borrow their gorgeous daughter Kiera, who always stole the show. My father's presence during the shoot is something I treasure. And to the rest of my family who were not able to be in Mauritius at that time—you were truly missed, and you had better be there for book two!

– Alicia Rountree

First published in the United States of America in 2020 by
Rizzoli International Publications, Inc.
300 Park Avenue South
New York, NY 10010
www.rizzoliusa.com

Foreword: Glenda Bailey
Texts: Alicia Rountree with Caitlin Leffel
Photography: Dewey Nicks
Photography assistance and styling: Shawn Merz
Hair and Makeup: James Michael Butterfield

Publisher: Charles Miers
Editor: Sandy Gilbert
Design: CHD Ltd
Production Manager: Barbara Sadick
Managing Editor: Lynn Scrabis
Editorial Assistance: Elizabeth Smith, Hilary Ney,
and Molly Ahuja
Design Coordinator: Olivia Russin

Furniture and tablesettings styling: Virginie Dalais at
Euphoria, Yuni Furniture & Lifestyle, and Anne Bedel
Hotels: Lux* Grand Gaube, Lux* Le Morne, Salt of Palmar
Clothing and jewelry: Adriana Degreas, Alicia Swim, Clube
Bossa, Harem Bath, Miguelina, Oceano Pearls

Photographic retouching: Gemma Bell and Mark Cossins
of Spring Studios
Production: Andreas Habermeyer of Identical Pictures
Recipes (adaptations for *Fresh Island Style*): Chef Khader
of Salt of Palmar—pages 52, 53, 73, 76; Salt of Palmar
team—pages 96, 188; Chef Fabio (in collaboration with Alicia
Rountree) of Spring Place—pages 28 (smoothies), 99, 116,
164 (juices, with the exception of Watermelon Refresher)

Printed in Italy

2020 2021 2022 2023 / 10 9 8 7 6 5 4 3 2 1
ISBN: 978-0-8478-6423-2
Library of Congress Control Number: 2019953109

Visit us online:
Facebook.com/RizzoliNewYork
instagram.com/rizzolibooks
twitter.com/Rizzoli_Books
pinterest.com/rizzolibooks
youtube.com/user/RizzoliNY
issuu.com/Rizzoli

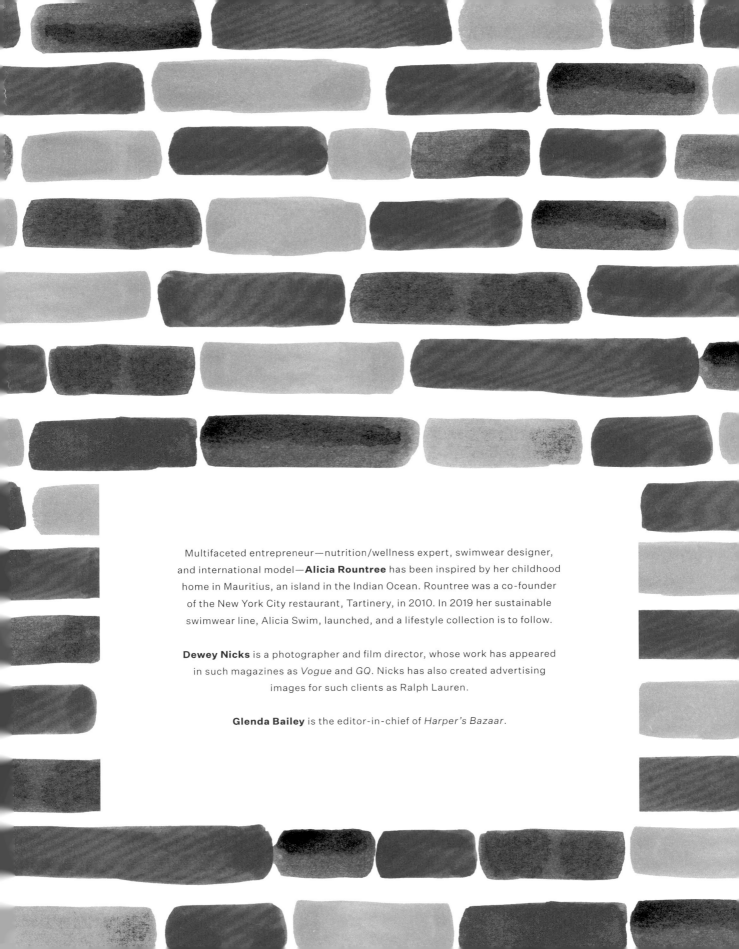

Multifaceted entrepreneur—nutrition/wellness expert, swimwear designer, and international model—**Alicia Rountree** has been inspired by her childhood home in Mauritius, an island in the Indian Ocean. Rountree was a co-founder of the New York City restaurant, Tartinery, in 2010. In 2019 her sustainable swimwear line, Alicia Swim, launched, and a lifestyle collection is to follow.

Dewey Nicks is a photographer and film director, whose work has appeared in such magazines as *Vogue* and *GQ*. Nicks has also created advertising images for such clients as Ralph Lauren.

Glenda Bailey is the editor-in-chief of *Harper's Bazaar*.